597

Wake Up to the World of Science

KU-072-077

FRESHWATER FISH
B. Bornancin

 *Burke Books* ▶B LONDON * TORONTO * NEW YORK

First published in the English language 1984
© Burke Publishing Company Limited 1984
Translated and adapted from *Poissons des eaux douces*
© Editions Fernand Nathan 1984

Acknowledgements
The publishers are grateful to Anne-Elise and Robert D. Martin for preparing the text of this edition, and to the following for permission to reproduce copyright illustrations:
    Chaumeton; Coleman: Burton; Labat; Nature: Aucante, Berthoule, Sauer, Siegel; Oxford Scientific Films; Zefa: Staenmans.

The drawings are by M. Campan.

CIP data
Freshwater fish. − (Wake up to the world of science)
        1. Fish, freshwater.
        I. Bornancin, B.   II. Poissons des eaux douces. *English*
        III. Series
        597.092'941   QL633,G7
        ISBN 0 222 01048 7
        ISBN 0 222 01049 5 Pbk.

Burke Publishing Company Limited
Pegasus House, 116 − 120 Golden Lane, London EC1Y 0TL, England.
Burke Publishing (Canada) Limited
Registered Office: 20 Queen Street West, Suite 3000, Box 30, Toronto, Canada M5H 1V5.
Burke Publishing Company Inc.
Registered Office: 333 State Street, PO Box 1740, Bridgeport, Connecticut 06601, U.S.A.
Filmset in "Monophoto" Souvenir by Green Gates Studios, Hull, England.
Printed in the Netherlands by Deltaprint Holland.

CONTENTS

Freshwater Environments

Freshwater environments can take a number of forms, including streams, rivers, ponds and lakes. They accordingly provide a variety of living conditions for the thousands of fish species that inhabit them.

Even a single river varies from its source to its mouth. A series of different zones can be identified along the course of a river, as shown in the table on page 5, though there is obviously a gradual change from one zone to another. Every type of fish occupies a particular part of the river according to the preferred water conditions and the availability of suitable food – algae, water-plants, larvae, small crustaceans, worms, etc. And many fish are preyed upon by other animals (predatory fish, birds, snakes and carnivorous aquatic mammals, such as the otter). Fry (young fish) are readily eaten by dragonfly larvae and by water-bugs (b).

Fish are, of course, often included in the human diet. At the right time of the year you yourself may catch some to eat.

Fish are particularly threatened by the pollution of inland waters and it is necessary to keep a careful check on the purity of water-courses. Nowadays, there are strict limits on the amount and type of industrial waste which factories may release into inland waterways.

A kingfisher, feeding on young trout

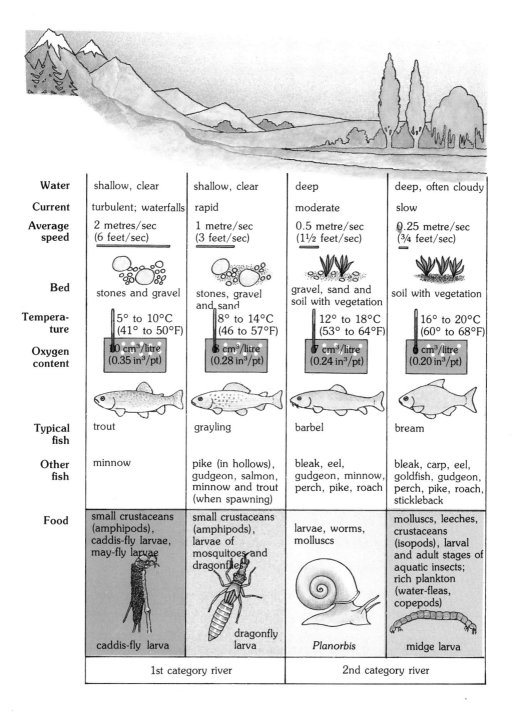

Water	shallow, clear	shallow, clear	deep	deep, often cloudy
Current	turbulent; waterfalls	rapid	moderate	slow
Average speed	2 metres/sec (6 feet/sec)	1 metre/sec (3 feet/sec)	0.5 metre/sec (1½ feet/sec)	0.25 metre/sec (¾ feet/sec)
Bed	stones and gravel	stones, gravel and sand	gravel, sand and soil with vegetation	soil with vegetation
Temperature	5° to 10°C (41° to 50°F)	8° to 14°C (46 to 57°F)	12° to 18°C (53° to 64°F)	16° to 20°C (60° to 68°F)
Oxygen content	10 cm³/litre (0.35 in³/pt)	8 cm³/litre (0.28 in³/pt)	7 cm³/litre (0.24 in³/pt)	6 cm³/litre (0.20 in³/pt)
Typical fish	trout	grayling	barbel	bream
Other fish	minnow	pike (in hollows), gudgeon, salmon, minnow and trout (when spawning)	bleak, eel, gudgeon, minnow, perch, pike, roach	bleak, carp, eel, goldfish, gudgeon, perch, pike, roach, stickleback
Food	small crustaceans (amphipods), caddis-fly larvae, may-fly larvae — caddis-fly larva	small crustaceans (amphipods), larvae of mosquitoes and dragonflies — dragonfly larva	larvae, worms, molluscs — Planorbis	molluscs, leeches, crustaceans (isopods), larval and adult stages of aquatic insects; rich plankton (water-fleas, copepods) — midge larva
	1st category river		2nd category river	

1. Compare the upstream part of a river (near its source in the *hills or mountains*) with the downstream part (in the *valley* close to the river mouth). What are the differences?

2. How can you show quite simply that water contains dissolved gases?

Naming Some Common Freshwater Fish

First of all, it is important to learn the names of the various parts of a fish, as indicated in the diagram. Once this has been done, it is possible to recognise the distinctive features of individual kinds (species) of fish.

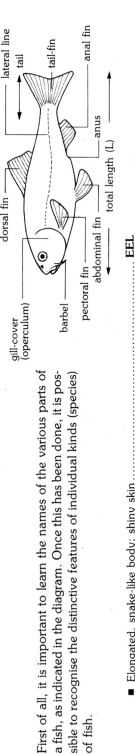

dorsal fin
tail
lateral line
tail-fin
anal fin
anus
total length (L)
abdominal fin
pectoral fin
barbel
gill-cover (operculum)

- ■ Elongated, snake-like body; shiny skin .... **EEL**

- ■ Typical fish-shape:

  - □ 2 dorsal fins

    - ● Without spines

      - a. ○ First dorsal fin long; small mouth; L = 30 – 50 cm (12 – 20 in).. **GRAYLING**

      - b. ○ First dorsal fin normal; large mouth

        - ● Straight tail; wide; L = 20 – 100 cm (8 – 40 in) .... **TROUT**

        - ● Indented tail; narrow in front; L = 50 – 150 cm (20 – 60 in) .... **SALMON**

      - ● First dorsal fin spiny, L = 20 – 50 cm (8 – 20 in) .... **PERCH**

  - □ 1 dorsal fin with free-standing spines in front; L = 5 – 8 cm (2 – 3 in) .... **STICKLEBACK**

  - □ 1 dorsal fin

    - a. ○ Dorsal fin located to the rear of the body; flattened snout; prominent teeth in mouth; L = 30 – 100 cm (6 – 40 in) .... **PIKE**

    - b. ○ Dorsal fin farther forward

      - ● Barbels present
        - — Long distal fin, large scales; L = 30 – 50 cm (12 – 20 in) .... **CARP**

        - — Short dorsal fin

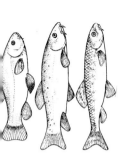

~~Bulky, shiny body, thick straight tail,~~
L = 30 – 50 cm (12 – 20 in) .... **TENCH**

+ Spindle-shaped body

  1. Elongated head with 4 barbels;
    L = 20 – 150 cm (8 – 60 in) .... **BARBEL**

  2. Short head with 2 barbels;
    L = 8 – 15 cm (3 – 6 in) .... **GUDGEON**

● Barbels absent

— Large body, indented tail

  + Back humped; long anal fin;
    L = 20 – 50 cm (8 – 20 in) .... **BREAM**

  + Back lower; fins and eyes reddish;
    L = 15 – 30 cm (6 – 12 in) .... **ROACH**

— Body slender

  + Silvery; large scales;
    L = 10 – 20 cm (4 – 8 in) .... **BLEAK**

  + Dark coloration; fine scales;
    L = 7 – 10 cm (3 – 4 in) .... **MINNOW**

The grayling (left): This silvery-grey fish is distinguished by its high dorsal fin. It seeks out cold, clear stretches of water and can withstand strong currents. Like the trout, which is found in the same regions of rivers, it is prized by anglers

The barbel (right): The barbel lives in small schools in clear, relatively calm patches of water. During the daytime, these fish keep still on the river bed, in the hollow of a water-fall, in the shadow of a bridge or at the edges of eddies. At night, they set out alone to find their food: molluscs, insect larvae, fish eggs, etc. Have you spotted the four barbels that give this fish its name?

An Aquarium for Freshwater Fish

It is a good ideal to set up an aquarium so that you can watch the fish at close quarters. You will need a tank with a rectangular base measuring about 50 × 80 cm (20 × 32 in). Do not use a spherical goldfish bowl, it will simply distort your view.

The first step is to prepare the base layer in the tank. For this, you need some sand, some gravel and a few assorted rocks. Wash them carefully and spread them over the floor of the aquarium . Then pour in a small amount of water, allowing it to flow down a sheet of glass (a) so as not to disturb the sand. Plant two or three clusters of green plants (waterweed, water milfoil, pondweed or the like) in a small amount of soil (b). These plants are needed not only to decorate the aquarium but also to enrich the water oxygen.

You can now add water until the tank is about three quarters full. As a final touch, you should add a thermometer (c) and perhaps an aerator. (You can buy these in an aquarium shop.)

When it is ready, the aquarium should be placed in a spot which is well lit but not directly exposed to the sun. Otherwise the sun might heat the water and kill the fish.

The first animals to be added should be pond-snails (*Limnea* and *Planorbis*), which will browse on algae that begin to grow on the glass walls of the tank.

Before any fish are introduced, you should wait a few days to let the tank settle down and reach a steady temperature. Then you can release some goldfish and you might even like to add some minnows, gudgeon or other suitable fish. Do not forget to cover the aquarium with a pane of glass to stop the water evaporating and to prevent the fish from escaping.

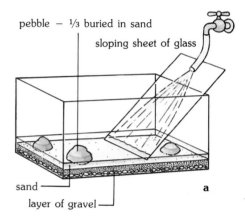

pebble – ⅓ buried in sand

sloping sheet of glass

sand

layer of gravel

a

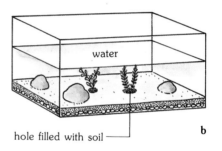

water

hole filled with soil

b

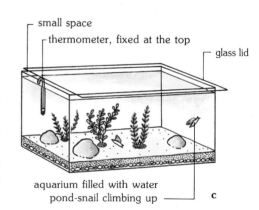

small space

thermometer, fixed at the top

glass lid

aquarium filled with water

pond-snail climbing up

c

The fish should be fed with dried water-fleas (from an aquarium shop) and small worms — scattered around in a single small quantity every day. Never put breadcrumbs into the water, as they easily begin to ferment. All the food should disappear within an hour after feeding. If any is left over, you have given too much! . . . and the excess must be removed.

If you follow these instructions carefully, you should not need to change the water in the aquarium. However, should it become necessary to change the water, follow the advice given below:

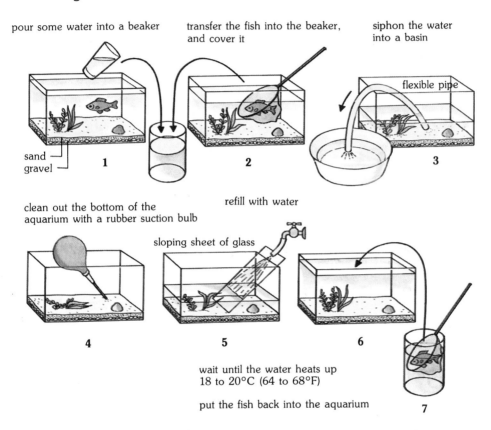

pour some water into a beaker

transfer the fish into the beaker, and cover it

siphon the water into a basin

flexible pipe

sand
gravel   **1**

2

3

clean out the bottom of the aquarium with a rubber suction bulb

refill with water

sloping sheet of glass

4

5

6

wait until the water heats up 18 to 20°C (64 to 68°F)

put the fish back into the aquarium   **7**

Once your fish are well installed, try to find out as much as you can about their life and about their remarkable adaptations for a watery environment.

The Goldfish

This common fish, which (despite its name) is rarely gold in colour, originated in Asia. Goldfish have been bred in China for eight centuries and were first introduced into Europe in 1750. They are now found living free in ponds and canals. You can easily obtain half a dozen goldfish, which you can then watch carefully in your aquarium.

Movements

The fish move smoothly through the water. They can move up or down and sometimes they appear to "tread water". Watch the body and the fins closely as the fish moves in different ways. When it moves forward rapidly, the tail beats. During slow swimming, the pectoral and abdominal fins seem to be used like oars; the fins move in a similar way even when the fish is not moving through the water, apparently to maintain its position.

Swimming depends upon the powerful muscles that are distributed along the body of the fish.

Feeding

You will soon realise that some fish prefer to take their food during slow, meandering movements over the bottom of the aquarium, while others continually move up and down, snapping up their food in the water. Droppings can often be seen coming out of the anus.

Goldfish feed on tiny animal prey and plant fragments. If you give them food at the same time every day, they will become accustomed to swimming up to be fed; they may even take the food out of your hand!

Breathing

Fish, of course, are almost always in the water. How do they breathe there? Look carefully at a fish, and you will notice regular movements of the mouth and gill-covers. You can carry out a very simple experiment. If you squirt a droplet of methylene blue (completely harmless!) in front of the fish's mouth, what happens? Bluish water comes out from the slit behind each gill-cover. The fish is continually pumping water over the gills located beneath the gill-covers (opercula). The gills, which are bright red in colour *(see the photograph)* have many blood-vessels. They extract oxygen dissolved in the water and discharge carbon dioxide produced as a result of activity. Fish are able to remain permanently underwater because of the availability of oxygen in solution. Dissolved oxygen is usually present in water, though the concentration of the gas depends upon the temperature *(see the table on page 5)*.

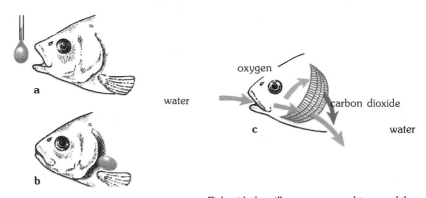

Fish with the gill-cover removed to reveal the red gills

Fish Sense

If you tap on the glass walls of an aquarium, the fish inside will become agitated. What produces this effect? In fact, if you look closely you can see a line of small dots running along each side of the fish's body. This is the "lateral line system", which contains tiny sense organs that respond to any vibrations passing through the water. In addition, the nostrils of the fish can detect smells; and their large eyes (which have no lids) can monitor movements and also, to some extent, shapes and colours. Goldfish seem to be interested in unfamiliar objects. For example, if you place a ring on the floor of the aquarium, these fish will come and investigate it.

Breeding

It is extremely unlikely that you will be able to observe breeding of goldfish in your aquarium. However, the breeding habits of the goldfish are very similar to those of the closely related carp *(see page 22)*. The freshly hatched fry are very pale in colour and only become coloured at about 3 to 4 weeks of age.

3. Make a drawing of a goldfish. Label all of the main organs that you can recognise and explain their function.

The Gudgeon

The gudgeon – note its short head and its barbel (it has 2 but only one is visible here)

The gudgeon is a small fish, about 8 – 15 cm (3 – 6 in) in length with a greenish-brown back and a silvery belly. It always stays close to the gravel bed of the rivers it inhabits.

This fish feeds on insect larvae, worms, small crustaceans and even the eggs of other fish which it finds in the gravel.

Breeding takes place in May and June. At this time, the male (barely different from the female for the rest of the year) develops dark spots on the head and front part of the body. Schools of gudgeon collect in quiet, relatively shallow places. Each female lays between one and 3,000 eggs in batches on the stones and plants on the river bed and the males discharge their sperm to fertilize the eggs.

The eggs, which are 2 mm ($^1/_{10}$ in) in diameter, take 10 to 30 days to hatch, according to the water temperature. The freshly hatched offspring remain at the site of hatching, close to the river bed.

You can catch gudgeon by fishing with a small worm or a maggot attached to the hook. These fish can be kept in a well-aerated aquarium, with small pieces of worm or meat provided as food.

In its natural habitat the gudgeon is preyed upon by carnivorous fish such as the pike, by certain birds such as the heron and the kingfisher, and even by grass snakes. Gudgeon lucky enough to escape these predators can reach three years of age.

4. How can you quickly tell the difference between a small gudgeon and a minnow?

The Minnow

This is a small grey fish with darker markings, apart from males during the breeding season. (They adopt a reddish tinge and are therefore brighter in appearance.)

The minnow inhabits fast-flowing, cool water-courses where the oxygen content of the water is quite high and where they are regularly taken as food by trout. Minnows move around in small schools accompanied by young trout and salmon of similar size.

The minnow is itself a voracious predator. It maintains a steady position against the current and eats any animal prey of suitable size (fish fry, worms, larvae, aerial insects, crustaceans) as well as some plant food.

At the beginning of summer, minnows gather together in large numbers to breed. The females have distended bellies and lay up to 1,000 eggs on the gravel of the river bed. Incubation of the eggs takes 6 days, but the subsequent development of this small fish is very slow: at one year of age, it is only 4 cm (1½ in) long.

This fish is particularly sensitive to the slightest trace of pollution. Dying minnows provide an alarm signal indicating that a river is under threat.

Gudgeons and minnows can both be caught with very simple fishing tackle:

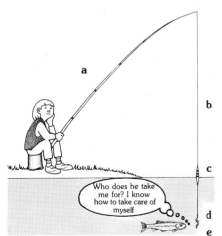

Who does he take me for? I know how to take care of myself

- a bamboo rod or a reed approximately 4 m (12 feet) long (a)
- 30 metres (90 feet) of line (b)
- an easily visible float (c)
- a fine hook (No. 18 or 20) (d)
- suitable bait (maggots; earthworms, freshwater worms)

 # The Trout

The trout − note the two dorsal fins, straight tail, spotted body and scales. Its colour varies according to the environment: a river trout is more brightly coloured than one which lives in a lake

The trout prefers cold, clean water with a high oxygen content *(see page 4)*. It is therefore commonly found in mountain streams and in unpolluted rivers.

This is a very agile fish, capable of swimming at speeds of 10 to 20 km/h (6 − 12 mph), and is the fastest swimmer among freshwater fish. Trout are most active when the water temperature is between 5° and 10°C (41° and 50°F). If the temperature rises above this level, trout become inactive.

The trout prefers a solitary existence and defends a territory. It feeds upon quite large animal prey (particularly minnows, insects and larvae) that are stalked and then swallowed whole. Indeed, it is even capable of devouring smaller or less agile trout. Small insects flying close to the water surface are also eaten frequently. When trout eat insects in this way, they are said to be "on the rise" and if you watch carefully you will be able to see them doing this in the river.

The spawning season is at the beginning of winter. At this time, trout have to seek out colder stretches of water with a higher oxygen content. Each female sets off to lay her eggs, followed by a number of males. Egg-laying takes place at night and the large eggs, measuring 4 to 6 mm (about $^1/_5$ in) across, are amber yellow in colour. The eggs are not laid all in one batch; instead they are laid in small numbers in different places at intervals of several days. A trout weighing 1 kg (just over 2 lb) can lay 2,000 eggs in this way. The males release their sperm in a white cloud over the eggs in order to fertilize them.

The eggs laid by the female are immediately fertilized by the male

The period of incubation of the eggs is usually quite long and depends upon the water temperature, taking 1½ months in water at 10°C (41°F). The fry are 1½ to 2 cm (½ to 1 in) long when they hatch and each one possesses a small bundle of reserve food in a vitelline sac, which gradually disappears (see page 16).

The small trout feed on plankton and grow at a rate of about 1½ cm (½ in) a month. Their rate of growth is really quite slow.

Subsequently, growth becomes even slower. In mountain lakes, some specimens may live up to 5 years, eventually reaching a length of 1 metre (3 feet) and a weight of 15 kg (33 lb).

Fish farms breed a less demanding trout species – the rainbow trout – which grows more rapidly. They reach a weight of 250 g (about 1½ lb) by two years of age and are then suitable for sale.

5. Compare the life of a trout with that of a carp.

The Hatching of a Trout

The process of hatching in the trout is shown in the following photographs, which are enlarged (as indicated in brackets).

a (× 6)

b (× 6)

● Look at the shape and colour of the fertilized eggs (a). They look like yellow, transparent balls. Note the fat droplets present in the eggs and the "dark spots" which are present to varying degrees. On some eggs it is possible to see a crescent-shaped red patch. Development takes several weeks then the fry emerges from the eggs (b) head first. The well-developed fry is shown in photograph c.

c (× 9.5)

● The fry swimming **(d)**. Its body is almost transparent. Try to trace the origin of the sac (vitelline sac) present beneath its body

● The ten-day-old fry; the vitelline sac is much smaller **(e)**

● Young trout. The vitelline sac has completely disappeared. They feed on plankton **(f)**

Not all fertilized eggs get as far as hatching! Far from it. It has been calculated that only one egg in 400 completes its development. Losses are very heavy because many eggs and fry are eaten by predators or succumb to the rigours of the environment.

There are many fish that breed in the same way as the trout. However, each species exhibits special features in the size of its eggs, their colour, the period of incubation, and so on.

6. Note the enlargements of the first three photographs and work out the actual size of the egg.

7. Observe a freshly hatched trout. What are the "black spots" in the first photograph? What function is served by the vitelline sac?

17

A NEST-BUILDING FISH

 # The Stickleback

The stickleback is a small fish between 5 and 8 cm (2 and 3 in) long. Its body is covered with bony plates

The stickleback lives in water with plenty of vegetation, in rivers and on the coasts, feeding on fish eggs, fish fry and small crustaceans. In its turn, the stickleback is preyed upon by salmon, eels and other fish.

This is a very lively fish, darting through the water like an arrow and even leaping out of the water quite frequently! The stickleback is quite aggressive by nature and when aroused it raises its spines and changes colour so that its jaws and belly look red! Fighting sticklebacks clash in an "upright" position, with their heads inclined downwards and their bellies touching. However, they rarely injure one another.

In spring, at the start of the breeding season, each male takes on a bright coloration and seeks out a territory in which it can construct a nest. The male first makes a small hollow in the sandy river-bed and then piles up successive layers of plant material (leaf fragments, roots, algae) that are anchored to surrounding vegetation with slimy mucus discharged from the anus. The end result is a small bundle about the size of a walnut. The male then makes an opening with a thrust of his head and the nest is ready. Once this is done, he looks out for a female to lead to the nest. When the female is in the nest, the male nibbles at her tail. In response, she lays about 100 eggs. Then he nudges the female out of the nest and swims through it himself to fertilize the eggs. This whole process can be repeated a number of times and the nest may eventually contain several hundred eggs that take about ten days to hatch.

a. Construction of a nest by the male

b. Courtship display

c. Female entering the nest

d. Male nibbling the tail of the female

Left on his own, the male vigorously defends his territory and makes sure that the water around the eggs is aerated by making fanning movements with his pectoral fins at the entrance to the nest. When the fry hatch, they are guided by their father, who brings back any strays in his mouth. After a few weeks, the young sticklebacks disperse in small groups.

Note how the male stickleback gathers material for nest-building

The Pike

The pike - note its dorsal fin well to the rear and its flattened snout

The pike leads a solitary existence in the still waters of lakes, ponds with really clean water, and slow-moving, meandering rivers. It seeks out places with a dense plant cover which allow it to hide and lie in wait for its prey. The pike only shows itself when it dashes out after small fish which attempt to escape by leaping out of the water.

This predatory fish has a whole battery of sharp, pointed teeth on its jaws and palate. Note the way in which it seizes its prey sideways on before swallowing it. The pike eats all kinds of fish (bleak, gudgeon, roach, etc.), insect larvae, frogs and even small water-birds. By eliminating weak and sick fish, and by chasing off other pike that stray into its hunting territory, this predator plays an important part in maintaining the natural balance of the river.

In winter, the pike often becomes more darkly coloured and takes refuge in holes. When the snows begin to melt in March and April, pike stop feeding and seek out

shallow water, especially in flooded meadows. Here the females lay a large number of eggs in several batches, approximately 20,000 eggs for every kilogram (2 lb) of body weight. The eggs are about 2½ to 3 mm ($^1/_{10}$ in) in diameter and are fertilized by the males after the females have spawned. Incubation takes about 12 days and the eggs then hatch to produce fry only 9 mm ($^1/_3$ in) long. The fry have no mouth and at first remain attached to nearby plants. The mouth opens only at the end of the first week after hatching and the young pike then begins to feed on small planktonic animals such as water-fleas and copepods. A month later, the growing pike measures 4 to 5 cm (about 2 in) in length and it then begins to prey upon the fry of other fish — tadpoles and the like. Thereafter, even larger fish are taken as prey. Pike reach adulthood at two to three years of age and live for about twelve years. Males never exceed one metre (3 feet) in length and the maximum weight is about 10 kg (22 lb). Females can reach 1 metre 30 cm (4 feet) in length and may weigh as much as 25 kg (55 lb).

Pike are themselves preyed upon by larger pike, by herons, by otters — and by anglers, who regard them as a particular delicacy.

A pike grasping its prey sideways.......

....he then turns it round and swallows it - headfirst

8. An angler has just caught a pike. Try to work out the original source of this tasty dish and make a sketch of the food-chain of the river.
9. Which of the fish described in this book have fry that are eaten by young pike in June?

21

The Carp

The carp was originally found only in Asia. It was probably introduced in to Europe by the Romans about 2,000 years ago. This fish is at home in stagnant (still) water that is relatively warm and low in oxygen content *(see page 4)*. It is widely bred in natural and artificial ponds.

Carp are most active during the summer months when the water temperature rises to between 15 and 25°C (59 and 77° F). Usually, they are lazy swimmers, but they can reach a speed of 8 km/h (5 m.p.h.) on occasions. Swimming carp betray their presence by brushing against water-lilies and thus producing ripples at the water surface. These fish have a hearty appetite, swallowing large quantities of tiny crustaceans (water-fleas, copepods, isopods), insect larvae, water-bugs *(Notonecta),* molluscs, worms, fish fry, fish eggs, seeds and plant fragments. In short, the carp will eat virtually anything - it is an *omnivore.* All the food that is taken is ground up by a battery of teeth located at the back of the mouth.

Carp require warm conditions for breeding. Spawning only takes place when the water temperature reaches at least 20°C (77°F). The eggs laid by the female are very small, measuring only 1 mm across ($^1/_{25}$ in), but they are produced in

large numbers. A carp weighing 1 kg (about 2 lb) can lay 100,000 eggs. The male discharges a cloud of sperm near the eggs in the usual way, but many of them remain unfertilized.

A few days after laying, the eggs hatch to release small fry measuring 6 to 8 mm (¼ to ⅓ in) in length. The vitelline sac *(see page 16)* rapidly disppears. The fry feed upon tiny animal prey and grow rapidly. At the age of two years, a well-fed carp will weigh about 1 kg (2 lb).

If the temperature falls below 15°C (59°F), the carp take much less food and they stop feeding altogether at temperatures less than 10°C (50°F). From October to March, they remain still and hidden (without feeding) at the bottom of the pond, where the water is warmer than at the surface. As a result, a fine growth ring appears on the scales each winter *(see the photograph)*.

A carp that manages to avoid various lurking predators (herons, water rats, otters) can reach an age of 30 years, with a body length of 70 cm (28 in) and a weight of up to 16 kg (33 lb).

Note the large scales on the body of the carp, and the barbels

10. Compare the life of the carp with that of the trout.
11. How may eggs can be laid at one time by a carp weighing 5 kg (10 lb)? Will all the eggs hatch? What might limit the number that hatch?

STILL WATERS

Bream

You can easily recognise this fish from its "humped" back! It seeks out the muddy bottom to feed on worms, flat pond-snails (planorbids) and isopod crustaceans. The prey are taken by the bream with its body standing almost vertically in the water!

In winter, bream gather together in schools to await the spring in deep water. Breeding takes place at the end of spring, with the fish gathering in boisterous groups near the banks.

Perch

This is an elegant fish in its greenish suit with black stripes! Note the spiny dorsal fin and the sharp tip on the gill-cover.

Perch live in groups in lakes, ponds and even rivers. Spawning takes place in April, in deep water with dense vegetation. The eggs are laid in ribbons, wrapped around plants and stones. After hatching, the fry feed upon insect larvae, crustaceans and the fry of other fish. When they grow older, they hunt for bleak and roach. A perch can reach the ripe old age of 15.

Bleak

Bleak swim around in schools beneath the well-lit water surface along the shores of lakes or by the banks of gently-flowing rivers. They feed on water-fleas, on mosquito larvae and on flying insects which they snatch just above the surface of the water. The main predators of bleak are perch and pike.

Spawning takes place in very deep water at the end of June.

Roach

This fish is very common in lakes and rivers, where it is caught by anglers. It is preyed upon by pike, eels, perch and herons.

Roach feed upon insect larvae, amphipod crustaceans, pond-snails (Limnea) and water-plants.

Spawning takes place in spring. The slimy eggs attach themselves to plants and stones on the bottom.

Tench

Look closely and note the bronze-coloured sides, the two barbels, the dark, rounded fins and the high-standing tail of this fish.

During the summer, tench seek out stretches of water with plenty of vegetation and sunlight, where they forage in the muddy bottom, which is rich in insect larvae and molluscs. You can see where tench are feeding: streams of bubbles rise to the surface at that spot. During winter, the tench bury themselves in the mud.

Breeding takes place in spring. The female lays more than 300,000 eggs, which stick to underwater plants.

Tench are often bred in ponds alongside carp.

The Eel

The male eel can grow to a length of 50 cm (20 in); the female to 100 cm (40 in)

Eels are found in almost all ponds and rivers. When it rains heavily, they will often leave their normal haunts and you may find them wriggling across flooded meadows. They can even be found in wells. Eels can survive well out of water because their gills are protected by a gill-cover with only a very small opening. When night falls, eels move about stealthily in search of their prey: small fish (such as the stickleback), frogs, crustaceans, worms, insect larvae, etc. During the daytime, however, they hide coiled up under rocks.

When the weather turns cold with the approach of winter, these fish become inactive. They hibernate in the mud, where they are protected from frost. With the arrival of spring, the eels wake up with their voracious appetite restored.

After several years have passed, when the eels are between the ages of four and eight, they develop a silvery colour on their bellies and, during October, instead of slowing down in preparation for hibernation, they become more active. They then set off downriver, without spending any more time feeding. In the estuaries and coastal waters, the females meet the males, which are smaller in size. Soon afterwards, before the end of October, the eels set out, usually by night, in large groups on an enormous voyage. They swim at great depths across the Alantic Ocean until they reach the Sargasso Sea in the Caribbean *(see map)*.

During their voyage, the eels travel about 20 to 40 km (12 to 25 miles) a day and, in the process, they lose about a quarter of their body weight. In fact, many of them die on the way. As eels travel, their sex organs develop. When they arrive at the Sargasso Sea, they are ready to breed. The females lay vast numbers of eggs (more than 1,000,000 each) which are fertilized in the open water by the males. After spawning, the adults die,

Elvers

the eggs develop to hatch out tiny, flat, transparent larvae only 5 mm (¹/5 in) long which feed on plankton. Over a period of three years during which they grow continuously, these larvae are carried along by sea currrents to the North Atlantic. Off the coast of Europe, they change their shape (undergo metamorphosis) to become small, transparent eels, some 6-7 cm (2½ in) in length. At this stage, they are know as elvers.

The elvers reach the coasts of Europe and North Africa in winter or spring and they head for the mouths of rivers. Some (the males) stay at the river mouths, while others (the females) head upstream. As they travel, their backs become darker in colour and their sides become yellowish.

Growth is slow in the rivers and this is why it takes a total of 4 to 8 years before the eels change in colour again to develop the silvery sheen on their bellies before returning to the sea.

This remarkable voyage remained completely unknown until the eighteenth century, but it is now well established that these migrations are an essential feature of the life of the eel − a fish which is born at sea, feeds and grows in estuaries and rivers, and returns to the sea to breed.

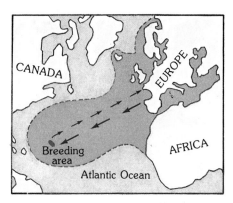

⟵ Adults on the way to the breeding area
→ → Larvae on their way to Europe
Eels in the sea

12. If an eel weighs 2 kg (4 lb) originally, how much will it weigh on arrival in the Sargasso Sea?
13. What is the distance covered by an eel during its migration through the Atlantic Ocean?
14. Why is it that we never find organs containing eggs or sperm (roe) in an eel caught in a river?

The Salmon

Salmon - superb, powerful fish - leave the sea in spring in groups of about 40 to make their way upriver. At this time, they have considerable fat reserves and they are much prized by anglers.

Salmon swim upstream against the current, leaping over obstacles as high as 2 to 3 metres (6 to 9 feet) on the way. They rest from time to time, but they do not feed. In fact, a kind of hook grows on the lower jaw of the male and this would get in the way during feeding. The spectacular voyage upstream continues until December, by which time the fish have reached relatively shallow, clear streams that are suitable as breeding-grounds. At this stage, the salmon take on a dark coloration with pink spots.

The male begins by digging a long trench in the gravel or sand of the stream bed. The female than lays 8,000 to 20,000 pea-sized eggs, in small batches. The eggs are fertilized by the male and then covered with sand or gravel. They are heavier than water and somewhat sticky, so they stay trapped in the stream bed throughout the winter.

The long upstream climb, without food, followed by spawning, exhausts the resources of the salmon, which lose 30 to 40 per cent of their body weight in the process. Many of them die, especially the males. The survivors spend the winter in deep patches of water or return immediately to the sea. Some of them will

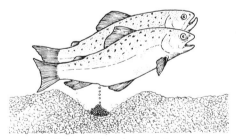
Male and female spawning

return to spawn a second time; and, in rare cases, a third such journey will be made.

The fry (alevins) hatch in April and May. They are about 2 cm (1 in) long and each one has a large vitelline sac (see page 16) which will provide food for about six weeks. After that, they hunt for mosquito larvae, small worms and other animal prey.

The young salmon grow slowly at the breeding-site; at the age of one year, they measure 6 to 8 cm in length (2½-3 in). At two years of age, they have reached a length of about 15 cm (6 in) and weigh about 40 g (1½ oz). This is the age at which they start to swim downstream to reach the sea. Their sides become silvery and covered with bluish spots, and they are now known as "smolts".

Note the two dorsal fins. It is not always easy to tell a young salmon from a trout

When they reach the river mouth, the smolts stay there in groups for a while to become accustomed to the salt water. Then they set out for the ocean depths, where they will find plenty of food: small fish, fish fry and other prey. Once there, they grow rapidly, putting on 2 to 4 kg (4 to 8 lb) a year.

After two to three years of life in the sea, an irresistible instinct drives the salmon to return to the original river to spawn. They are guided by a very delicate sense of smell that permits them to identify the odour of the waters in which they were born. By attaching identification rings to individual salmon, it has been shown that they have made enormous journeys, covering a distance of 50 to 100 km (30 to 60 miles) in a day.

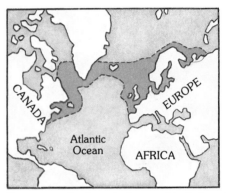

Occurrence of salmon in the sea (shaded area)

This migratory fish, with its unusal habits, is now severely threatened. Since the beginning of the twentieth century, as a result of industrial development, water pollution has become widespread and many dams too high for the salmon to jump have been constructed. In Europe, numerous breeding-sites for salmon have been destroyed. At the beginning of this century, 7,500,000 salmon arrived in the Baltic Sea every year; but this figure had fallen to 2,000,000 by 1970. Conservation measures are urgently needed to stop any further decline in the salmon population.

15. Imagine a river in which a salmon has just hatched. Make a sketch of the travels of this fish. Indicate where it grows and where it breeds, and show where it grows the fastest.

Answers to questions

Freshwater Environments

1 page 5 Changes in a river between upstream and downstream:
- There is a decrease in altitude and the speed of flow of the water declines
- The temperature of the water increases, while the amount of oxygen decreases *(see page 5)*
- The density of the vegetation increases

2 page 5 If you heat the water in a saucepan, you will see bubbles of gas escaping. Therefore the water must contain dissolved gases that are invisible to the eye.

The Goldfish

3 page 11 The Gudgeon and the Minnow

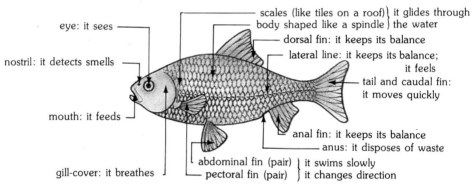

eye: it sees

nostril: it detects smells

mouth: it feeds

gill-cover: it breathes

scales (like tiles on a roof) \ it glides through
body shaped like a spindle / the water

dorsal fin: it keeps its balance

lateral line: it keeps its balance; it feels

tail and caudal fin: it moves quickly

anal fin: it keeps its balance
anus: it disposes of waste

abdominal fin (pair) \ it swims slowly
pectoral fin (pair) / it changes direction

The Gudgeon and the Minnow

4 page 13 The young gudgeon has 4 barbels; the minnow has none.

The Trout and the Carp

5 page 15

		CURRENT	OXYGEN	TEMPERATURE OF MAXIMUM ACTIVITY
LIVING CONDITIONS	TROUT	very rapid	10 cm³/l (0.35 in³/pt)	5-10°C (41° – 50°F) 15 – 25°C (59° – 77°F)
	CARP	slow	6 cm³/l (0.20 in³/pt)	below 8°C (46°F), the carp hibernates

6 page 17 The average size of the egg is 0.5 cm (¼ in)

7 page 17

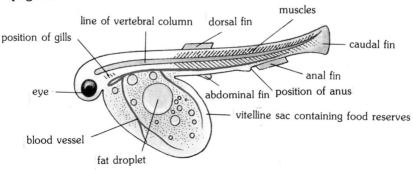

position of gills

line of vertebral column   dorsal fin   muscles

caudal fin

eye

anal fin

abdominal fin position of anus

vitelline sac containing food reserves

blood vessel

fat droplet

The Pike

8 **page 21** A food-chain in the river

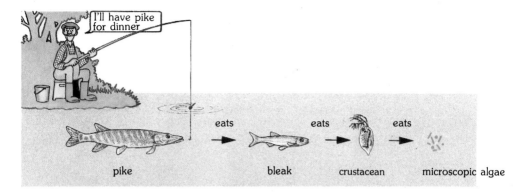

9 **page 21** The young pike lives in still water and feeds upon the fry of fish that live there: bream, carp, tench, roach. These fish lay large numbers of eggs in spring, with the result that there is an abundance of fry in May and June to provide food for the young pike.

The Carp

10 **page 23** See answer to question 6

11 **page 23** A carp weighing 5 kg (10 lb) can lay 5 times 100,000 eggs, that is a total of 500,000 eggs. Not all of the eggs will hatch. The eggs and the fry are preyed upon by numerous aquatic animals (insects, fish, birds).

The Eel

12 **page 27** An eel weighing 2 kg (4 lb) at the beginning of its migration in the sea loses a quarter of its body weight, that is 0.5 kg (over 1 lb). Thus, it will only weigh 1.5 kg (3 lb) on arrival in the Sargasso Sea.

13 **page 27** The eel travels 30 km (20 miles) a day on average. The voyage takes 6 months, or about 180 days. Thus, the total distance travelled across the Atlantic is 5,400 km (3,380 miles).

14 **page 27** The sex organs are only developed during the sea migration.

The Salmon

15 **page 29** Environment, growth and reproduction

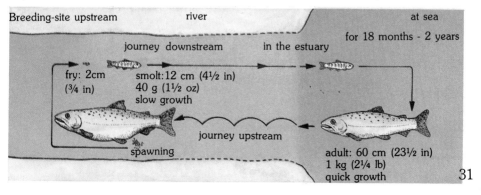

INDEX